A Note From Rick Renner

I0200878

I am on a personal quest to see a "revival of the Bible" so people can establish their lives on a firm foundation that will stand strong and endure the test when the end-time storm winds begin to intensify.

In order to experience a revival of the Bible in your personal life, it is important to take time each day to read, receive, and apply its truths to your life. James tells us that if we will continue in the perfect law of liberty — refusing to be forgetful hearers but determined to be doers — we will be blessed in our ways. As you watch or listen to the programs in this series and work through this corresponding study guide, I trust that you will search the Scriptures and allow the Holy Spirit to help you hear something new from God's Word that applies specifically to your life. I encourage you to be a doer of the Word that He reveals to you. Whatever the cost, I assure you — it will be worth it.

> Thy words were found, and I did eat them;
> and thy word was unto me the joy and rejoicing of mine heart:
> for I am called by thy name, O Lord God of hosts.
> — Jeremiah 15:16

Your brother and friend in Jesus Christ,

Rick Renner

Unless otherwise indicated, all scripture quotations are taken from the *King James Version* of the Bible.

How To Improve Family Relationships

Copyright © 2020 by Rick Renner
8316 E. 73rd St.
Tulsa, Oklahoma 74133

Published by Rick Renner Ministries
www.renner.org

ISBN 13: 978-1-68031-711-4

eBook ISBN 13: 978-1-68031-712-1

How To Use This Study Guide

This five-lesson study guide corresponds to *"How To Improve Family Relationships" With Rick Renner* (Renner TV). Each lesson in this study guide covers a topic that is addressed during the program series, with questions and references supplied to draw you deeper into your own private study of the Scriptures on this subject.

To derive the most benefit from this study guide, consider the following:

First, watch or listen to the program prior to working through the corresponding lesson in this guide. (Programs can also be viewed at **renner.org** by clicking on the Media/Archive links.)

Second, take the time to look up the scriptures included in each lesson. Prayerfully consider their application to your own life.

Third, use a journal or notebook to make note of your answers to each lesson's Study Questions and Practical Application challenges.

Fourth, invest specific time in prayer and in the Word of God to consult with the Holy Spirit. Write down the scriptures or insights He reveals to you about being filled with the Spirit and empowered by Him in your daily life.

Finally, take action! Whatever the Lord tells you to do according to His Word, do it.

For added insights on this subject, it is recommended that you obtain Rick Renner's book *Dream Thieves: Overcoming Obstacles to Fulfill Your Dreams.* Denise Renner's books *Who Stole Cinderella?* and *The Gift of Forgiveness* would also be greatly beneficial. You may also select from Rick's other available resources by placing your order at **renner.org** or by calling 1-800-742-5593.

TOPIC

Improving Relationships Between Husbands and Wives

SCRIPTURES

1. **Galatians 6:7** — Be not deceived; God is not mocked: for whatsoever a man soweth, that shall he also reap.

2. **Proverbs 14:1** — Every wise woman buildeth her house: but the foolish plucketh it down with her hands.

3. **Hosea 4:6** — My people are destroyed for lack of knowledge.

4. **Proverbs 19:13** — The contentions of a wife are a continual dropping.

5. **Ephesians 5:25** — Husbands, love your wives, even as Christ also loved the church, and gave himself for it.

6. **1 Peter 3:8** — Finally, be ye all of one mind, having compassion one of another, love as brethren, be pitiful, be courteous.

7. **1 Peter 3:9** — Not rendering evil for evil, or railing for railing: but contrariwise blessing; knowing that ye are thereunto called, that ye should inherit a blessing.

8. **Romans 12:18** — If it be possible, as much as lieth in you, live peaceably with all men.

9. **Ecclesiastes 3:5** — A time to embrace, and a time to refrain from embracing.

10. **Ecclesiastes 3:7** — A time to keep silence, and a time to speak.

SYNOPSIS

Family relationships are some of the most precious relationships you'll ever have in this life. Therefore, it's important to take care of the people in your home and learn to communicate with them according to the Word of God. The home is the building block of society, and the marriage union is the foundation of the home. Because husbands and wives are at the core of all relationships, strengthening the marriage union is a critical responsibility for all couples. By taking simple steps to improve your relationship with your spouse, you can plant good seeds towards your marriage and ultimately reap a bountiful harvest of love, kindness, peace, and joy in your home.

The five lessons in this series include detailed discussion on the following family-relationship topics:

- Improving Relationships Between Husbands and Wives
- Improving Relationships Between Parents and Children
- Improving Relationships Between Siblings
- Improving Relationships With Parents
- Improving Relationships With Older Parents

The emphasis of this lesson:

The relationship between husband and wife is the most precious human relationship you can ever have on this earth. By learning how to properly cultivate the ground of your marriage, you can reap a wonderful marriage full of God's many blessings. Sowing the right seeds in your marriage begins with taking responsibility to build your house instead of tearing it down. It also requires a proper understanding of one another as members of God's family and being sensitive to each other's needs. When you begin to hear and do the Word, and sow good seeds into the ground of your marriage, you will reap a harvest of a long, happy marriage that fulfills God's purposes on earth!

You Reap What You Sow

Every marriage has the potential to produce fruit in each season of life. However, marriage requires intentionality and deliberate action to nurture the relationship into something precious and beautiful. No matter where you are in the marriage journey, you can apply the Word of God to your home and take the relationship with your spouse to the next level. God's Word will strengthen you, fortify you, and transform your marriage from one season of glory to another.

The key in taking your relationship to the next level in God's plan is contingent upon the seeds you sow into your marriage. Galatians 6:7 says, "Be not deceived; God is not mocked: for whatsoever a man soweth, that shall he also reap." The law of seedtime and harvest applies to every arena of life — and your marriage union is no exception!

The condition of a marriage is the result of what a couple puts into it. If someone constantly sows bitterness, strife, or hurtful words, then it should not be a surprise when the marriage itself becomes bitter and harsh. On the other hand, if a husband and wife continue to sow time, love, and attention towards one another, then their marriage will produce a harvest of love and blessings. Whatever one sows is what one will reap.

A Word to Wives: Build Your House

Ladies, the Bible has some special instructions for you in Proverbs 14:1: "Every wise woman buildeth her house: but the foolish plucketh it down with her hands." As a wife, you have the option to either build up or tear down your own house. The choice and responsibility are yours.

If you desire to build up your house, you need God's wisdom to help you in the process. As Denise likes to say, "There really aren't bad wives, but ones who perish because of a lack of knowledge." Ladies, you need knowledge and wisdom from the Lord to help you build up a strong marriage and family that can withstand all of life's storms.

Many women tear down their homes through simple ignorance of God's Word. They build their homes from the traditions handed down to them from their mothers and grandmothers; they may even build from something they read in a magazine or heard from a friend. But the most truthful and correct instruction comes from the Bible. A woman who is building her family to endure in any environment is one who has learned to go to God first and receive His distinct blueprint for her home. It is this approach to marriage and family that will create strong homes in the Body of Christ.

When a woman doesn't build her home on the Word of God, she may encounter hardship in her marriage or with her children. However, it's important to note that when challenges come, a woman can't throw all the blame onto her husband, her mother-in-law, or her kids. She has a part to play in determining the condition of her family. The Bible reveals her personal responsibility to build her house and create the right environment in her home.

One common challenge many women experience is a tendency to complain or nag their husbands or children. The Bible says the contentions of a wife are like a continual dripping of a faucet (Proverbs 19:13). Whenever you have a leaky faucet, the first thing you want to do is turn it off! No one wants to listen to the constant annoying drip, drip, drip of water hitting the bathroom sink. Unfortunately, that's what you become when you continually complain, criticize, or find fault with your husband and family. Your voice and actions become nothing more than the irritating sound of a leaky, drippy, worn-out, rusted faucet.

Thankfully you can control the words and attitudes coming out of your mouth. You don't have to be the leaky water spout. Instead, you can add value to your home and become a healthy plumbing system by continually expressing words of love, kindness, and thankfulness to those around you.

Understandably, your husband will make mistakes. No one is perfect, and he is accountable before God for the choices he makes. However, you have the responsibility to withhold verbal fault-finding, criticism, and judgment. Instead of pointing fingers at him every time, take these issues before the Lord and earnestly pray for your husband. Allow the Spirit of God to work inside both of your hearts as you grow closer together in your marriage union. If you will be intentional in sowing good things in your family relationships — peace instead of contention, forgiveness instead of offense, and patience instead of nagging — you can build up a strong and beautiful home that will last for many years to come!

A Word to Husbands: Love Your Wives

Men, God has some special instructions for you in Ephesians 5:25: "Husbands, love your wives, even as Christ also loved the church, and gave himself for it." One of the primary responsibilities God has given you as a husband is to simply love your wife. However, this can become a challenge if you don't properly understand your wife. Because women are created very differently from men, they respond and communicate in very different ways, which can cause friction and frustration in the marital relationship.

When you are unsure of how to properly love and care for your wife, the Bible has some words of wisdom for you. First Peter 3:8 says, "Finally, be ye all of one mind, having compassion one of another, love as brethren, be pitiful, be courteous." The last phrase "love as brethren" means to love one another as brothers and sisters in the Lord. Whenever you are getting frustrated with your wife, your conversation with her is turning heated, or you don't understand what she's saying, just take a step back from the intensity of the moment. Change your perspective and see her as a sister in the Lord. This revelation will help you engage with her in a more loving and patient manner.

Long before you married your wife, she was first your sister in the Lord. In fact, your marriage is only a short-term, earthly relationship in light of the long-term, eternal relationship of the family of God. Your marriage has purpose here on this earth, but when you die and go on home to heaven, you will remain brother and sister in the Lord. This is a precious reality for the saints in God.

When you begin to see your wife as not only your partner in this life but also as your sister in the Lord, you will discover a newfound level of patience and courteousness towards her. Any sister in the Lord deserves respect and honor — even in difficult moments. Would you constantly correct every sister in the Lord? Hopefully not. In the same way, you should not correct your wife at every opportunity either. By honoring her as a sister in the Lord, you are honoring the most eternal part of your relationship.

Here's another piece of instruction for you men: Don't get into the business of payback. First Peter 3:9 says, "Not rendering evil for evil, or railing for railing: but contrariwise blessing; knowing that ye are thereunto called, that ye should inherit a blessing." In other words, don't retaliate. Whenever your spouse insults you, respond with a blessing instead of another evil or snide remark. Keep the peace in your home and don't fall into the trap of payback!

Romans 12:18 says, "If it be possible, as much as lieth in you, live peaceably with all men." These instructions include your spouse. God wants you to do whatever you can to live at peace with your wife. When you make that commitment to maintain peace in your home, you will find that keeping your mouth closed is worth the price of peace and contentment with your wife.

Another piece of advice for you men is to learn to give your wife some space when she needs it. Ecclesiastes 3:5 teaches that there is: "A time to embrace, and a time to refrain from embracing." Ecclesiastes 3:7 states there is: "A time to keep silence, and a time to speak." Sometimes your wife needs you to just listen to her, not fix her problem. Other times she may need you to hold her closely, or she may need you to go to another room in the house for a while. Whatever the situation may be, learn to read your wife and be flexible with her emotions and needs. Ask the Lord to help you understand your wife and be sensitive to what she needs from you and when.

Finally, the most important key to improving your relationship with your wife is spending time with God. When you spend time with the Lord, God will speak to your heart. He'll show you how to act towards your wife, how to lead your home, and how to be a father to your children. He sees both your blind spots and the needs of your family members. He is faithful to show you how to be the man He wants you to be and how to lead your home with tender love and godly strength.

Examine Your Harvest

The Biblical law of sowing and reaping cannot be violated. Whatever you sow into your marriage is what you will reap. What you do for your spouse may determine what your spouse does for you. What you sow into your spouse may determine what kind of harvest you reap back from your spouse. Your marriage is, and always will be, a result of the seeds you sow into the ground of your relationship.

If you feel like you're in the middle of reaping a bad harvest, take some time to examine the seeds you've been sowing for the past few years. What can you do differently to elevate the status of your relationship? What kind of good seeds do you need to start planting to create a better harvest? How can you change the course of your relationship so you and your spouse both produce sweet fruit in your marriage?

After honestly examining your field, determine in your heart to be a hearer and doer of the Word. Ladies, take responsibility to build up your home instead of tearing it down with your words and attitudes. Men, honor your wife as your sister in the Lord and be sensitive to her needs. As you both prioritize your relationship with the Lord, allow the Holy Spirit to deal with your hearts and show you areas you need to change. Together, you can sow good seeds towards your marriage and reap a bountiful, beautiful harvest of love, joy, and peace in your home!

STUDY QUESTIONS

Study to shew thyself approved unto God, a workman that needeth not to be ashamed, rightly dividing the word of truth.
— 2 Timothy 2:15

1. Proverbs 14:1 says, "Every wise woman buildeth her house: but the foolish plucketh it down with her hands." Ladies, what are you doing today to build up your house?

2. Ephesians 5:25 says, "Husbands, love your wives, even as Christ also loved the church, and gave himself for it." Men, how are you showing love to your wife today?

3. Romans 12:18 says, "If it be possible, as much as lieth in you, live peaceably with all men." What can you do to increase the peace in your home?

PRACTICAL APPLICATION

But be ye doers of the word, and not hearers only,
deceiving your own selves.
—James 1:22

Improve your relationship with your husband or wife by sowing good seeds into your marriage.

1. Ladies, examine the words that come out of your mouth when you speak to your husband. Do you sound like a drippy faucet, or are your words full of grace and forgiveness? How can you adjust your attitudes to reflect godly character?

2. Men, take a moment to examine how you treat your wife. Do you get mad and blow up when you don't understand her? What can you do differently to show patience and tender love to your wife when you don't agree?

3. What is the current state of your marriage harvest? Is it good? Does it need some work? How can you start sowing better seeds into the ground of your marriage to produce a healthy harvest?

TOPIC

Improving Relationships Between Parents and Children

SCRIPTURES

1. **Galatians 6:7** — Be not deceived; God is not mocked: for whatsoever a man soweth, that shall he also reap.

2. **Galatians 6:9** — And let us not be weary in well doing: for in due season we shall reap, if we faint not.

3. **Hosea 4:6** — My people are destroyed for lack of knowledge.

4. **Ephesians 6:1-3** — Children, obey your parents in the Lord: for this is right. Honour thy father and mother; which is the first commandment with promise; That it may be well with thee, and thou mayest live long on the earth.

5. **Romans 12:10** — Be kindly affectioned one to another with brotherly love; in honour preferring one another.

SYNOPSIS

Parenting is one of the most important responsibilities a person can have in this lifetime. However, parenting is not for the faint of heart! It requires grace, patience, wisdom, good communication skills, and a high degree of adaptability. In its challenging moments, parenting can often become confusing and frustrating — for both the adults and the kids! Thankfully God's Word provides powerful instruction for building strong families that overcome difficulties and glorify God. When parents determine to plant the right kinds of seeds into the hearts of their children, they can grow a beautiful garden full of faith, character, love, and immense joy.

The emphasis of this lesson:

The relationships between parents and children is a precious gift in the Body of Christ. In order to improve these relationships, it's critical to understand the principle of seedtime and harvest—whatever a parent sows into the life of their child is what they will reap in years to come.

Being intentional to plant the right kinds of seeds into children when they're young is key to harvesting many years of healthy family life in the future. By understanding how God made their kids and taking the God-given responsibilities of parenting seriously, parents can enjoy every moment of this wonderful season in life.

Be Intentional in Sowing Towards Your Children

Your children are like a garden, and the fruitfulness of your family is dependent upon the seeds that you sow into this area of your life. If you want a bountiful harvest of love, closeness, peace, and joy in your relationships with your children, then you will need to sow the appropriate seeds. Sowing towards your family doesn't come easily or by chance; intentionality is required if you desire the right kind of harvest.

Galatians 6:7 explains the divine law of seedtime and harvest: "Be not deceived; God is not mocked: for whatever a man sows, that shall he also reap." The Greek emphasizes this point by saying that a man reaps whatever he *sows and sows and sows and goes on continually, habitually sowing.* In other words, your harvest is the result of whatever seed you consistently and intentionally sow on a regular basis. If you plant good things, you'll reap a great harvest; if you plant bad things, you'll reap a bad harvest. This is an unshakeable law of the kingdom of God.

Perhaps you're a parent who may not be satisfied with the current harvest in your children. Maybe you've been trying to plant good seeds, but you haven't seen the results you desire yet. Regardless of where you are in your parenting journey, you can start sowing good seeds into your children more consistently and intentionally. Your seeds *will* eventually produce a harvest!

Galatians 6:9 gives this powerful piece of encouragement: "And let us not be weary in well doing: for in due season we shall reap, if we faint not." The word "faint" in the Greek means *to give up and give out.* God absolutely promises that if you'll be consistent in sowing the right kinds of seeds into your children, in due season you will reap if you don't faint, don't give up, and don't give out. You may be tempted to quit or throw in the towel, but don't give up! Continue doing what is right and in due season you will reap a marvelous harvest in your children.

While parenting is a precious calling, it can be difficult for people to know how to parent their children properly and how to plant the right kinds of seeds into their kids. Parents may have a poor harvest in their kids because they've sown the wrong seed. They may make mistakes in their parenting because they are modeling what their parents taught them.

Thankfully, God has a manual for parents in His Word. The Bible says in Hosea 4:6, "My people are destroyed for lack of knowledge." God doesn't want you to be ignorant of godly parenting principles, and He knows the secrets needed to raise your children in the right way. If you will go to the Lord in prayer and seek counsel from His Word, He will illuminate your pathway.

Your parenting journey doesn't have to be a frustrating or unfulfilling one. With God's wisdom and instruction, you *can* be equipped to sow the right kinds of seeds into your child's life. You *can* raise kids who become responsible, mature, and loving. Your children *can* grow up to be a blessing to you in your later years, and you *can* enjoy a sweet relationship with each one of them if you are intentional with the seeds you plant in them while they're young.

However, if you're not intentional about the seeds you sow, you can produce kids who will end up depending on you for the rest of their lives. Instead of being a blessing, they'll become a curse to you. A lack of intentionality now can create a nightmare later!

If you're parenting kids who are still at home, be encouraged. While the road may seem challenging at times — especially if you're the parent of younger children — remember to be intentional in the seeds you are sowing. Be consistent every single day. Those long days with your children will go by quickly, and you have but a small window of time to build a strong foundation in them for the future. As you intentionally plant good seeds into their lives every day, you can rest assured that in due time you will reap a beautiful harvest in your children.

You Are Responsible To Understand and Teach Your Children

Your children are uniquely created by God with special gifts, tempera-ments, and personalities. Because no two children are exactly the same, it's important for you to understand the key differences and purposes God has for each one of them. Perhaps one child is athletic and another is artistic; one may be self-corrective and the other strong-willed. No matter what kind of temperament your child possesses, it's your responsibility as a parent to nurture him in the ways of God without comparison or prejudice.

In order to properly guide and direct your children, you need to study them. This requires prayer and careful observation of each child in your home. Some things they do may not make sense to you, but if you see your children in the light of God's unique design, you'll begin to understand them. When you pray and seek the mind of God for every child, the Lord will show you how to teach them, train them, and prepare them for their own God-designed purpose.

Of course being a parent can be frustrating at times — especially when there is a breach in understanding. When it seems like something you're saying is not getting through to your children, take a step back and explain yourself. Take every moment as a teaching moment. Remember, your children are children. They are not adults yet, and they do not understand things at your level of comprehension. Be patient with them in the process and ask the Holy Spirit to open the eyes of your understanding so you can make the most of each opportunity to teach and train your children.

Sometimes the breach of understanding happens when you don't understand what your children are trying to communicate to *you*. Children are in the process of growing and learning. They may not yet know how to properly control their emotions or express themselves in an appropriate way. To you, it may look like they're being disobedient or angry, but they may just be frustrated and don't know how to communicate what they're feeling. Whenever you feel like you're about to pull your hair out, take a deep breath, and calmly use that moment as an opportunity to help your child develop their communication skills and emotional maturity. You can say something like, "Let's talk about this. Tell me what you're trying to say." Help them explain themselves. By approaching your difficult parenting moments in this manner, both you and your children will benefit from these opportunities and grow together in your relationships with one another.

As a parent, your God-given role in your child's life is that of a teacher. You're not a commander angrily whipping them into shape. You're a teacher. And through your kindness, patience, and understanding, you are modeling the right kind of character in front of your children. You are sowing into them the right kind of seeds that will bear much fruit later in their life.

You Are Responsible To Discipline Your Children

As a parent, you are also biblically responsible to discipline your children. By training them and establishing rewards and consequences for certain types of behavior, you are disciplining them for a balanced and healthy adult life. Disciplining isn't always easy, but it's necessary for planting good seeds in the soil of your child's heart.

One area that requires your consistent discipline is teaching your children to respect authority. It's critical that you teach your children to respect authority on every level for this is key to success in life. If your children grow up to become disrespectful adults, they won't be able to keep a job or be promoted. They'll never do well in life and could even have trouble with the law. Therefore, it's extremely important for you to establish a healthy respect for authority in your children as early as you can. Teach them to respect authority, their elders, and their pastor. You won't regret this critical part of your parenting assignment!

When instructing your kids about authority, it's also important to teach them to respect the things of God. Take your kids to church, show honor to your pastor, read the Bible with them, and pray with them. Your kids are watching you all the time, and what you display in front of them is what they will remember. They will follow not just your words but also your personal example. If you treat the things of God without reverence, your children will do the same. When your kids see you reading your Bible or praying, you will give them a healthy dose of respect for God's Word. You sow seeds into your children's spiritual lives by taking your own relationship with the Lord seriously.

Honoring authority is a scriptural principle that governs the kind of harvest reaped. For example, Ephesians 6:1-3 says, "Children, obey your parents in the Lord: for this is right. Honour thy father and mother; which is the first commandment with promise; That it may be well with thee, and thou mayest live long on the earth." A long life on this earth is the harvest reaped from sowing seeds of honor to your parents. By teaching your children to respect authority, you are making it possible for them to live a long time on the earth. That is a promise of God!

You Are Responsible To Speak Correctly Over Your Children

Another important thing to consider in your parenting assignment is the responsibility you have before God to speak the right words over your children. Your words are like seeds, and when you speak words over your kids, you are planting things deep into the soil of their hearts. Refuse the temptation to speak bad words over your children — even during times of frustration or disappointment. Don't tell them that they're a mess or call them derogatory names. Determine to stay away from the comparison trap by comparing your children to other children. Instead, go to the Word of God and find promises to speak over your children. As you speak words of life and faith, you are planting good seeds in your children for a hopeful, faith-filled future!

Whenever you do find yourself saying something that's wrong over your child, be quick to apologize. If you get angry and say something hurtful, repent. Speak the truth to your child and be an example of humility and repentance. When your child sees you repent in front of them, you are teaching them how to repent. You are modeling godly behavior and planting the right kind of seeds into their little hearts.

Remember your children are not perfect. They have a lot of learning and growing to do while they're under your care. Your children are your seed — they bear your name, they carry your blood, and they're going to have your grandchildren. Treasure them! Express appreciation for what they do. Be generous and kind in your words towards them, for your words are like sweet rewards. Refrain from constant criticism and judgment; instead, be mindful of your attitudes and your words. Don't curse your children — bless them! It's ok for you to lighten up your expectations of them — they're a work in progress and need your tender love and patience as they grow into the people God has called them to be.

Your Children Are God's Gifts of Joy

Your children are one of the greatest gifts God gave you. In fact, children are created to bring an incredible amount of joy to parents and to the world. Have you ever noticed how funny kids are? They're creative and imaginative, and they enjoy the simplest of life's pleasures. They are part of the joy in life God has for you!

In improving your relationships with your children, remember that God invested these little ones into your care as a source of joy for you and your spouse. Instead of stressing out about your kids all the time, allow them to bring you joy. Laugh with them, play with them — just enjoy them!

Your kids will be kids for only a short while. The childhood season of life is fleeting in comparison to how long adult life lasts. So remember to take advantage of this time. Invest in making fun memories with them. Your season of parenting doesn't have to be so intense if you'll learn to appreciate the joy that God brings through the life of your children. Raise your children with a love for life so that one day they can say, "Oh, it was always so much fun to be with Mom and Dad."

Your Children Are Your Spiritual Family

Finally, it's important for you to recognize that your children are your spiritual family. They are your brothers and sisters in the Lord. The Bible is clear on how the family of God is to treat one another. Romans 12:10 says, "Be kindly affectioned one to another with brotherly love; in honour preferring one another." If you have children who are born-again, then they are part of your family in Christ and are to be treated as such with kindness. They deserve your respect because your son is also your Christian brother, and your daughter is also your sister in the Lord. In that light, you need to treat them with the same dignity that you would give to anyone else in the local church.

Whenever certain moments of parenting become challenging, take a step back and remember that your children are also your brothers and sisters in the Lord. You don't want to lose your temper with them and angrily say something that you'll regret later. It's ok to pause and step away from an emotionally-charged situation. During the pause, take a breath and get your emotions under control, then ask the Lord for His perspective and His help. By taking those challenging moments before the Lord, you have an opportunity to get God's mind on the matter. Then, when your emotions have calmed down, you can address the issue with clarity and anointing.

No matter where you are in your parenting journey, remember to keep sowing the right seeds. Don't give up when you become frustrated. Be intentional to cultivate the garden of your family. Take your responsibilities as a parent seriously, and ask the Lord to help you understand, teach, and discipline your children correctly. Speak the right words over your kids and treasure your time with them. If you'll be faithful to continue sowing and sowing and sowing the right seeds into their hearts, in due time, you will have a beautiful, fragrant garden in the lives of your children!

STUDY QUESTIONS

Study to shew thyself approved unto God, a workman that needeth not to be ashamed, rightly dividing the word of truth.
— 2 Timothy 2:15

1. Galatians 6:7 explains the divine law of seedtime and harvest: "Be not deceived, God is not mocked. For whatever a man sows, that shall he also reap." Parents, what kinds of seeds are you sowing into your children?

2. Ephesians 6:1-3 says this: "Children, obey your parents in the Lord: for this is right. Honour they father and mother; which is the first commandment with promise; That it may be well with thee, and thou mayest live long on the earth." Are you teaching your children to honor and respect authority so they can have a long and prosperous life?

3. Romans 12:10 says, "Be kindly affectioned one to another with brotherly love; in honour preferring one another." Have you ever considered your children as your brothers and sisters in the Lord?

PRACTICAL APPLICATION

But be ye doers of the word, and not hearers only, deceiving your own selves.
— James 1:22

Improve your relationships with your children by sowing good seeds into their hearts.

1. What has been your approach to parenting? Do you view it as an obligation or a joy?

2. In what ways are you intentional in sowing good seeds into your children's hearts? What are some areas you need to correct in order to sow better seeds for the future?

3. Are you modeling respect for the things of God in your home? How can you do better in this area in order to sow seeds of honor and respect into your children's hearts for God's Word, prayer, and church?

TOPIC

Improving Relationships Between Siblings

SCRIPTURES

1. **Galatians 6:7** — Be not deceived; God is not mocked: for whatsoever a man soweth, that shall he also reap.

2. **Galatians 6:9** — And let us not be weary in well doing: for in due season we shall reap, if we faint not.

3. **Romans 12:18** — If it be possible, as much as lieth in you, live peaceably with all men.

4. **Ecclesiastes 3:5** — A time to embrace, and a time to refrain from embracing.

5. **Ecclesiastes 3:7** — A time to keep silence, and a time to speak.

6. **Ephesians 4:31-32** — Let all bitterness, and wrath, and anger, and clamour, and evil speaking, be put away from you, with all malice: And be ye kind one to another, tenderhearted, forgiving one another, even as God for Christ's sake hath forgiven you.

SYNOPSIS

Sibling relationships are special and meant to be enjoyed. In fact, God wants people to laugh with their brothers and sisters and to take pleasure in these unique family relationships. When siblings grow up, leave home, get married, and make their own way in the world, relationships can often drift apart. Different perspectives and life experiences can make it even more difficult for siblings to connect. However, by following the law of seedtime and harvest, families can come together again and enjoy the fruits of genuine fellowship. Sibling relationships can be restored, and unity in the family can become a reality once again.

The emphasis of this lesson:

The relationships between siblings are like no other. However, different perspectives and life choices can create holes in sibling relationships, leaving both parties distant and uncommunicative. Thankfully there is a Biblical solution to restoring the closeness and fellowship in sibling relationships. By sowing the right kinds of seeds — understanding, forgiveness, acceptance, and peace — siblings can draw closer to one another and enjoy each other's unique graces and giftings. Challenging relationships can be restored, and peace can dominate the dynamics between brothers and sisters — even in adulthood.

You Reap What You Sow in Your Sibling Relationships

The Bible reveals an eternal principle of seedtime and harvest. Galatians 6:7 says, "Be not deceived; God is not mocked: for whatsoever a man soweth, that shall he also reap." When you sow seed, you will reap a harvest according to the kind of seed you sow. If you are a generous person, you'll reap generosity; if you show mercy to others, you'll reap mercy. If you sow forgiveness to someone, you'll harvest forgiveness from another. Whatever you sow, and continually sow, is what you will eventually reap.

When it comes to family relationships, the law of seedtime and harvest determines the kind of relationships you'll experience with those close to you. By sowing seeds of time, attention, love, patience, and forgiveness, you'll reap a harvest reflecting those qualities. On the other hand, if you sow bitterness, offense, jealousy, or strife, you will reap a crop of negative attitudes and behaviors. The condition of your relationships is up to you, and you can change the type of harvest you'll reap if you'll make a determined effort to sow the right kinds of seeds.

In sibling relationships, the principle of seedtime and harvest governs the outcome of these types of relationships as well. By planting the right seeds with your siblings, you will reap a good harvest, even if it takes a while. Eventually, you will reap if you faint not. If you don't like the harvest you have right now, take some time to examine the types of seeds you've been planting in the relationships with your siblings. You are living now what you've been planting in years gone by, and you will reap tomorrow the harvest of the seeds you are sowing today.

While this reality may be a little difficult to hear, it is Bible truth. It also will help you recognize where you need to take responsibility for the outcome of your relationships with your siblings. If you're not satisfied with the quality of your relationships, adjust what you're sowing. If you've been planting the right seeds but haven't seen the harvest you'd like, don't give up! By continuing to sow the right seeds into your relationships, you will reap the harvest you're looking for if you don't grow weary in well doing. You will reap if you faint not!

Understanding Sibling Differences

One thing that helps in planting the proper seeds in sibling relationships is to understand that you and your siblings are different. No two siblings within one family are the same. Every child grew up with his or her own rank in the home. The first child is different from the second, and the second is different from the third. As the parents age and adjust their parenting practices, they shape their children in unique ways. For example, people who are new to the role of parenting are often more strict with their firstborn. With the birth of the second child, they've learned the ropes and are often settling into a more relaxed parenting style. By the time the third child arrives, the parents are older and can be more lenient. As a result of all these changes the parents experience, each child is treated just a bit differently. It's no wonder that three siblings in the same house can turn out completely different from one another.

In addition to the changing dynamics within the family, individual giftings and temperaments also play a part in molding siblings. Each sibling is graced with different personalities, talents, experiences, and disappointments. Therefore, siblings will view everything with varying degrees of perspectives. The key to improving relationships between siblings is learning to appreciate the differences and accepting one another without judgment.

If you want to improve your relationships with your siblings and plant the right kinds of seeds into your relationships, you will need to sow the seed of understanding. Your siblings are unique from you and approach life in their own special way. Learn to honor them. Honor who they are and honor their gifts. Respect their opinions even if you don't agree with them. Just like you, they have a right to their own opinion. Respect their experiences in life. There's a reason why they think what they think. You may not agree with their decisions, but you need to respect them for the conclusion they've come to even if you see it differently. By sowing understanding, you are planting the right kinds of seeds into your sibling relationships — and when you need understanding from them, you will harvest it back because of the seeds you have sown.

Keep in mind that trying to change your sibling is never a good idea. Don't try to make them be like you, because they're not you! They will never be just like you, and they probably don't want to be like you. Allow them the freedom to be who God created them to be, which is someone completely different than you.

It is possible that you may have drifted from your siblings during your adult years. Many siblings are close during childhood but grow further apart as they move through adulthood. Once spouses come into the mix, the sibling dynamic changes even more as additional people are brought into the family. But remember this — even if relationships change, your siblings are still your siblings. It's important to embrace them for who they are today in this stage of life. Pray for your siblings. Be supportive of them. Don't be judgmental or nitpicky with them; instead, extend grace and understanding to all your family members. By believing the best of them, you are planting the right kinds of seeds into your sibling relationships.

Be Intentional

Another key to improving relationships with siblings is being intentional with them. You and your siblings may live on opposite sides of the world, but you are still family. It may take some concerted effort to keep lines of communication open, but the rewards will be great. Modern technology has made long-distance communication possible; you can call, text, Skype, email, or use social media. Your schedules may be crowded with other responsibilities, and it may be challenging to keep up the relationships when everyone has different jobs and other family priorities. However, if you will be intentional in communicating with your siblings, you can continue nurturing those relationships for years to come.

Intentionality is also required to walk in forgiveness with your siblings. Failure to extend forgiveness towards your brother or sister keeps you a prisoner and impedes genuine fellowship with one another. Therefore, consider Paul's words, "And be ye kind one to another, tenderhearted, forgiving one another, even as God for Christ's sake hath forgiven you"

(Ephesians 4:32). By sowing forgiveness, you will reap a rich reward in your family relationships!

Do Everything You Can To Live in Peace

As you go through life, you and your siblings will have different experiences and disappointments that may lead you in opposite directions. It's possible that your siblings don't even believe what you do anymore. You may really be living on two different pages! If that's the case, you need God's wisdom to know what to say and what not to say so you can maintain peaceable relations.

Taking issue with all your disagreements isn't a good idea nor is it profitable. If you know discussing a certain topic may lead to contention, it's best not to go there. You can choose from a variety of other safe subjects that won't steal the peace between you and your siblings. For example, you can talk about the fun memories you had as kids growing up together. You can talk about their children or hopes for the future. There are a lot of things you can discuss that won't lead to a fight.

In choosing the path of peace, learn to submit to the counsel of God's Word. Romans 12:18 says, "If it be possible, as much as lieth in you, live peaceably with all men." Make a commitment to do everything you can within your realm of responsibility to live at peace with your brother or sister. This sets a great example to all your family members of exemplifying Christ-like character in your home.

Recognize the Season of Your Relationship

You may feel like you've entered a tricky time in your relationships with your siblings. Perhaps a sharp disagreement has arisen in the family, or a certain event has complicated relational dynamics. In the event of special circumstances, it's important to heed the wisdom of God. The Bible speaks often of different seasons in life and relationships, and it's possible you may be in a delicate season with your siblings. Ecclesiastes 3:5 reveals there is: "A time to embrace, and a time to refrain from embracing."

Sometimes it's wise to back up from a contentious relationship and give your sibling some space. If your brother or sister is upset about something, give him or her time to cool off and think. You need time to reflect too! Ecclesiastes 3:7 states that there is: "A time to keep silence, and a time to speak." Occasionally, silence is really the best course of action.

Of course, it's always best when you can sit down and talk through your disagreements. But if your sibling is not willing to open his or her heart, listen, forgive, and come to a place of understanding and cooperation, it's wise not to push the issue. When a relationship reaches an impasse, the way of wisdom is to back up, and give each other space and quiet. This approach allows both of you to process the situation, pray about it, and come back for resolution at a future time. This ability to be sensitive to the season in your relationship will help you from planting the wrong kinds of seeds with negative attitudes, actions, and words.

Let God Work in Your Relationship

Finally, if you want to improve your relationships with your siblings, allow God to work in them and in you. In a time of disagreement or frustration, refuse to harden your heart towards your siblings. Always keep your heart open towards them and to what God can do in those relationships. The Holy Spirit is your Helper, and He can help you navigate through any challenges you may encounter in your sibling relationships. He will show you when you need to say something, and He'll show you when to remain quiet. He'll give you the right words to say at any moment if you'll listen to Him.

As you're following the Holy Spirit's leading in your relationships, remember these important words from the Apostle Paul: "Let all bitterness, and wrath, and anger, and clamour, and evil speaking, be put away from you, with all malice: And be ye kind one to another…" (Ephesians 4:31-32). That word "kind" in the Greek means *to be adaptable*. In other words, you need to be adaptable to your siblings. Don't always demand that your siblings be like you, meet your needs, or be what you think they should be. Instead, consider how you can adapt to your siblings. This character of kindness and adaptability is a fruit of the Holy Spirit and will produce a harvest of wonderful things in your life.

Paul continues in Ephesians 4:32, "…tenderhearted, forgiving one another, even as God for Christ's sake hath forgiven you." The word "forgiving" is from the word *charis*, which is the word for *grace*. In context, Paul is admonishing the Church to be graceful with one another. When applying this to your siblings, you can understand how God desires for you to extend grace to your brother or sister. Forgive them if they've hurt you or mistreated you. Give them the grace that they need for whatever it is they may be experiencing. Maybe they are going through some hard times right now, and what they need most from you is a little grace.

In the same verse, Paul also emphasizes the fact that God has graciously forgiven each one of us. The Greek word here for "forgiven" refers to that same favor and grace. So no matter what your siblings may have done to you in times past, just extend grace and let it go. Release it. Forgive them. Open the prison doors for yourself and for the relationships. Make the decision to forgive and let it go.

You might find forgiveness hard, especially if a sibling has deeply wounded you. However, you need to keep in mind just how much Jesus forgave you for your own trespasses and sins. There was plenty you did in the eyes of Jesus that was hurtful or ugly, yet God chose to forgive you fully and completely. This same power to forgive lives in you, and you can choose to forgive anyone who has ever wronged you. You are free to forgive!

When you forgive according to the Bible, you no longer hold that person's sin against them. You no longer recall the hurt, the ugly words, or the bad attitudes they might have held towards you. Instead, you can reach down deep in your heart and draw from the well of your own salvation — you can release your siblings in Jesus' name and let all the hurt, anger, and bitterness go. When you forgive, you never have to retrieve it again. It is permanently sent away and gone from you. You are free.

By releasing your siblings from things they did wrong to you, peace will come into your heart. You'll enter into a new time of peace and enjoyment with your siblings. God can work in a whole new way in your family, and your relationships with them can be restored.

Remember, you may have many friends, but you only have one, or just a few, siblings — they are your family. Be intentional in planting the right kinds of seeds into these relationships. Sow understanding, sow grace, sow forgiveness, sow peace, and sow acceptance. As you continue to sow good seeds, you will eventually reap an abundant harvest if you don't give up. God wants you to be able to laugh with your brothers and sisters. He wants you to enjoy one another. And through the Lord Jesus, you can enjoy your siblings like no one else on earth.

STUDY QUESTIONS

Study to shew thyself approved unto God, a workman that needeth
not to be ashamed, rightly dividing the word of truth.
— 2 Timothy 2:15

1. Galatians 6:7 explains the divine law of seedtime and harvest: "Be not
    deceived, God is not mocked. For whatever a man sows, that shall he
    also reap." What kinds of seeds have you been sowing in your rela-
    tionships with your sibling(s)?

2. Ephesians 4:32 says, "And be ye kind one to another, tenderhearted,
    forgiving one another, even as God for Christ's sake hath forgiven you."
    Have you been sowing kindness and forgiveness to your sibling(s)?

3. According to Ecclesiastes 3:5, there is: "...a time to embrace, and a
    time to refrain from embracing." Have you been sensitive to the dif-
    ferent seasons in your sibling relationships?

PRACTICAL APPLICATION

But be ye doers of the word, and not hearers only,
deceiving your own selves.
— James 1:22

**Improve your relationships with your siblings by sowing the right kinds
of seeds.**

1. Do you and your sibling(s) have a good relationship? What specific
    seeds can you sow that will make your relationship with each other
    stronger?

2. Have you held resentment or offense against one or more of your
    siblings? If so, take some time today to get quiet before the Lord and
    repent of your unforgiveness. Allow the Lord to wash you clean and
    create a right spirit within you. Let all unforgiveness, hurt, bitterness,
    or anger go.

3. What can you do today to be intentional in communicating with your
    sibling(s)?

TOPIC

Improving Relationships With Parents

SCRIPTURES

1. **Galatians 6:7** — Be not deceived; God is not mocked: for whatsoever a man soweth, that shall he also reap.
2. **Galatians 6:9** — And let us not be weary in well doing: for in due season we shall reap, if we faint not.
3. **Ephesians 6:2** — Honor thy father and thy mother; which is the first commandment with promise.

SYNOPSIS

Honor is key to improving relationships with parents. No home or parent is perfect, but most parents did the best they could to raise their children. At the very least, they fed them, clothed them, provided shelter, and sent them to school. Many parents also taught their children valuable lessons that prepared them for a successful adult life. All of these things are worthy of honor and respect. Just like anything else in life, when the seed of honor is sowed into a relationship, it will eventually produce a harvest of honor. Because the Bible says that honoring parents is the first commandment with promise, honor will produce rich rewards for those who develop this quality in life.

The emphasis of this lesson:

The relationships between parents and children is one that should be cherished and enjoyed. When children learn to honor their parents, they engage in a spiritual principle that will serve them well in life. While parents are not perfect, it's important to honor them for the good things they did, even if it was just meeting basic needs during childhood. Adult children can learn to forgive their parents' past mistakes and live in a place of freedom through obedience to God's Word. By honoring parents now, people can also sow into their own future, because their children will treat them later exactly how they treat their parents today.

What You Do Will Come Back to You

Every person has a choice as to what kinds of seeds he or she sows in family relationships; good seeds or bad seeds. Regardless of what kinds of seeds a person plants, he will eventually reap what he has consistently sowed. Everything in life has a cause and effect, and whatever a person does will eventually come back to him. The law of seedtime and harvest is an irrefutable law of the kingdom and cannot be changed.

People can grow weary in their season of planting. They can uproot their good seeds prematurely before they reap the harvest. This is why the Bible encourages believers not to grow weary in well doing. It takes time to reap a crop!

In applying the law of seedtime and harvest to family relationships, it's important to remember that what you sow in your relationships with your parents is what you will reap back with your own children later in life. If you sow honor, you will reap honor. If you sow mercy, you will reap mercy. If you sow forgiveness, you will reap forgiveness. Whatever you plant towards others is what you will harvest from them.

If you've been consistently planting the right kinds of seeds but haven't seen a harvest yet, you might be feeling a bit discouraged. But don't give up hope — the Bible says you *will* eventually reap from the seeds you have sown. If you keep investing correctly in a relationship, eventually all your labor is going to come back to you — and it's going to be so good! Just remember that your timing isn't God's timing. Don't give up before your harvest comes in — continue to sow and plant, sow and plant. Your sweet harvest will come if you will simply refuse to quit.

Honor Your Parents

One of the most important seeds you can sow into your relationships with your parents is honor. Ephesians 6:2 says, "Honor thy father and thy mother; which is the first commandment with promise." This principle of honor applies to you even if you think your parents aren't worthy of honor. No parent is perfect, but most parents try to do the best they can in raising their kids. It's true your parents might not have done everything right, but they are still your parents and worthy of honor.

Many parents reflect the imperfections passed on to them from their parents. Some fathers may be stern or disengaged simply because that's how their fathers were with them. A few mothers may have insecurity issues because they were raised in a broken home and were not properly affirmed by their fathers growing up. In any case, adults usually bring into their own parenting the examples they learned from their parents. Some may have grown up in godly homes where the Word of God was taught as the standard, while others may have grown up in a home where the Bible wasn't even opened.

No matter what mistakes your parents made, extend to them grace and forgiveness. Above all, honor them. Appreciate the effort they made to raise you, feed you, clothe you, and care for you while you were growing up. Many parents worked long hours to put food on the table and that is worth respect. Your parents may not have done everything right, but they probably did the best they could to make life good for you.

Remember the Good Your Parents Did

What you remember about your parents is a choice. You can dwell on all the wrong they did or you can be intentional to recall their best attributes. Maybe your father was stern, but he instilled a sense of personal responsibility in you. Perhaps your parents worked hard and missed a lot of events, but their hard-earned money paid for your food, shelter, and education. When you choose to focus on the positive instead of the negative, you'll find appreciation and respect growing in your heart towards your parents.

If you came from a troubled family, ask the Holy Spirit to help you see something that your parents tried to do right. Even if your parents didn't do their best, try to find something they did try to do and honor them for that. Find something they did right and be thankful for at least one thing. Your honor is a gift to them and it may open up a door for healing and restoration in your relationships.

Tell Your Parents Thank You

If you're still living at home or if you moved out of the house years ago, take time to acknowledge your parents' sacrifice for you. Tell them thank you for what they did. You may even want to make a list of all the things your parents have done for you over the years and share it with them. They spent a small fortune clothing and feeding you when you were younger. They made sure you had a bed to sleep in and a roof to cover your head.

Keeping you warm and safe and meeting your basic needs is worthy of gratitude. Thank them for that!

If your parents are alive, call them today. Tell them thank you for all they did to raise you, feed you, clothe you, and shelter you. You may also want to share with them some special memories or things you learned from them. Your parents won't be around forever and it's important you take the time to communicate your gratitude for them while you still have the opportunity.

Perhaps you may be thinking, "Well, my parents really didn't do a good job." In that case, forgive your parents for the mistakes they made. By forgiving them of all the hurt and pain they may have caused you growing up, you release yourself and the relationship from an emotional and spiritual prison. Bitterness and unforgiveness will damage your heart if left unchecked. In order to walk in freedom, you need to release your disappointments, anger, or wounds to the Lord. Uproot them from your heart. You don't have to live subject to your emotions and memories. You can command them to be uprooted and removed in Jesus' name. You may not be able to correct the past, but you can change your future. Allow the love of God to work in your heart, forgive your parents, and let it go.

Honor Is Not Based on Emotions

Many people mistakenly think they can only show honor when they feel good about a person but honor does not depend on emotions. Honor is a decision. Regardless of how one thinks or feels about someone, he can still show honor and proper respect towards that person.

Showing honor to your parents is critical for receiving honor from your own kids in the future. Because of the eternal law of seedtime and harvest, if you dishonor your parents, your children will eventually dishonor you. That's a serious situation!

However, you can plant wonderful seeds for the future if you'll commit to being a doer of the Word and honor your parents today. Remember the best of them, thank them for the good they did for you, and forgive them for their mistakes. By choosing to honor your parents, you will not only improve your relationships with them, but you will also create a good future for yourself and your children in the years to come.

STUDY QUESTIONS

Study to shew thyself approved unto God, a workman that needeth
not to be ashamed, rightly dividing the word of truth.
— 2 Timothy 2:15

1. Galatians 6:7 explains the divine law of seedtime and harvest: "Be
   not deceived, God is not mocked. For whatever a man sows, that shall
   he also reap." How are you sowing good seeds into your relationships
   with your parents?
2. Ephesians 6:2 says, "Honor thy father and thy mother; which is the
   first commandment with promise." Have you been showing proper
   honor to your father and mother?
3. Galatians 6:9 says, "And let us not be weary in well doing: for in due
   season we shall reap, if we faint not." Have you felt discouraged in
   planting good seeds towards your relationships with your parents?
   How will you continue to sow the right kind of seeds until you see
   your harvest?

PRACTICAL APPLICATION

But be ye doers of the word, and not hearers only,
deceiving your own selves.
— James 1:22

**Improve your relationships with your parents by sowing good seeds into
your relationships with them.**

1. Think about how you honor your mom and dad. Would you pass
   God's honor test in how you show your parents kindness and respect?
2. If your children treated you in the future the way you treat your parents today, would you be joyful or disappointed?
3. If you came from a troubled home, think of at least one good thing
   your parents did for you during your childhood. Consider calling
   them to share that memory and to express your gratitude.

TOPIC

Improving Relationships With Older Parents

SCRIPTURES

1. **Galatians 6:7** — Be not deceived; God is not mocked: for whatsoever a man soweth, that shall he also reap.

2. **Galatians 6:8** — For he that soweth to his flesh shall of the flesh reap corruption; but he that soweth to the Spirit shall of the Spirit reap life everlasting.

3. **Galatians 6:9** — And let us not be weary in well doing: for in due season we shall reap, if we faint not.

4. **Psalm 71:9** — Cast me not off in the time of old age; forsake me not when my strength faileth.

5. **Proverbs 23:22** — Hearken unto thy father that begat thee, and despise not thy mother when she is old.

SYNOPSIS

Taking care of the elderly is a biblical concept and command. The older years can often be difficult as mobility is hindered and loved ones die. During these later years, family members have an opportune time to show kindness and honor to their elderly parents. By remembering parents in their old age, believers are putting the Word into practice and sowing good seeds into their own future. The golden years can become a precious time for all when the law of seedtime and harvest is recognized and engaged!

The emphasis of this lesson:

The relationships between adult children and their elderly parents can be challenging; full of both grief and frustration. However, when believers understand what the Bible says about caring for elderly parents and the rewards that are associated with honoring them, this relational season can become one of the most precious and cherished of all. Adult

children have the opportunity to forgive parents, be a blessing to them in old age, treasure their advice, and affirm them in their twilight years. As a result of obedience to the Word, adult children can invest in their own future by planting seeds of honor in the lives of their elderly parents.

Don't Be Deceived

The Bible reveals an irrefutable law of the Kingdom — the law of sowing and reaping. This law cannot change for it has been established by God and reflects an eternal principle — whatever a person sows is what he ultimately reaps.

In relating to this principle, Galatians 6:7 states, "Be not deceived; God is not mocked." The words "be not deceived" mean *to not let anyone take you by the hand and lead you astray or off track*. In this case, the Bible is warning believers not to underestimate the power of sowing and reaping. Your words and actions matter, and they will come back to you just as you sowed them! The Bible is clear that whatever you sow — whether good or bad — has an effect. This principle can serve as both an encouragement and a warning, depending on what kinds of seeds you are sowing.

The law of seedtime and harvest is such an eternal principle that God said He can't be mocked in regards to it. In other words, you can't turn your nose up to God as if to say, "Ah, this works for everybody else but it has no application to me." You would be deceived believing such thoughts! God's Word works for everyone, and the laws of God always work. So when the Bible says you reap what you sow, you can bank on it! It will happen whether you like it or not and even if you agree with it or not. What you do is what will be done to you. Remember — it is an irrefutable law.

Galatians 6:9 goes on to say, "And let us not be weary in well doing: for in due season, we shall reap if we faint not." That's a promise! If you want a good harvest, you need to be sure you're sowing the right kinds of seeds. If you're currently living in a hard season, you're reaping the harvest from past bad seeds. Instead of blaming everyone else for your negative circumstances, take a look at yourself and ask, "What kind of seed did I sow in my life that I have reaped this kind of harvest?" When you honestly evaluate your field, you can take responsibility for past behavior and take it before the Cross. After repenting before the Lord, you can ask the Holy Spirit to help you plant the right kinds of seeds for a better outcome in the future. If you don't like your current harvest, start planting with a different kind of seed!

In applying this truth to your family relationships, it's important to think about the kind of harvest you want when you are older. Do you want to be lonely or forgotten in life when you reach your elderly years, or do you want to be loved and well taken care of? If you want your golden years to be your best years, then you need to start planting towards that kind of harvest. In other words, begin planting towards your future by taking care of your elderly parents now.

Based on the spiritual law of seedtime and harvest, how you treat your older parents is exactly what will come back to you when you are older. That's a powerful principle that will help guide you in your decisions, attitudes, and actions towards your elderly parents.

If you have older parents, value the time you have left with them. This is a precious season in which you can sow into them. Instead of resenting your responsibilities, appreciate your time together with them. Let this be a season to release any bitterness or offense you may have held towards your parents. Release any old, hurt feelings and forgive your mom and dad for any wrong they may have done to you. If you'll be consistent to sow the right kinds of seeds, your relationships with them can be restored. In fact, let this be an opportunity to take back anything the devil might have stolen from these relationships.

By understanding the law of seedtime and harvest, you can set the right course for your future. Don't regret this time with your elderly parents — take advantage of it! Love on them, forgive them, and let God heal any wounds in those relationships. As you commit to planting the right kinds of seeds towards your elderly parents, you will reap a harvest in kind from your children in the future.

Remember Your Parents in Old Age

Old age can be a difficult season for many. As people get older, they must adjust to losing friends, loved ones, and spouses. They may also lose their mobility, their community, and even their sense of freedom and independence. All of these changes can be extremely difficult as life becomes lonely, isolated, and inactive at that age.

When thinking about your elderly parents, listen to the counsel from Psalm 71:9: "Cast me not off in the time of old age; forsake me not when my strength faileth." It can be tempting to cast off or ignore your parents when they are elderly, but God wants you to care for them with His love. He wants you to remember them, to have compassion on them, and to be a support for them in their old age.

If you have parents who are older, take every opportunity you can to call them, connect with them, and check in on them. Visit them often and make time for them. Think about how you might feel when you are old and how you would want others to treat you. Wouldn't you want to be remembered and not forsaken? If you want your children to show you grace and love in your old age, start by doing the same for your elderly parents now. By remembering your parents in their old age, you are planting good seeds for your children to remember you.

Ignore and Be Ignored

Perhaps you came from a difficult family that didn't give you much growing up. More than likely, your parents did the best they knew how in raising you. If they could do it over again, they would probably do it better. But neither you nor they can reach back into the past and change it. What's done is done, and the only choice ahead of you is either to forgive them and plant the right kinds of seeds or to harbor unforgiveness and continue the cycle with your own children.

If you give in to negative feelings and ignore your parents, you are sowing bad seed. The law of sowing and reaping will come back to you, and you will be ignored in your old age. On the other hand, if you take care of your parents, the law of sowing and reaping will work for you and you'll be taken care of in your later years. You can determine your own future just by sowing the right kinds of seeds today.

Affirm Your Parents

When people get older and become more sedentary, they have a lot of time to sit and think. Sadly, these extended periods of contemplation can lead to a lot of negative thoughts and regrets. Older people tend to reflect on previous chapters in life and see a lot of their mistakes. They wonder about the choices they've made and what they could have done better.

This can be a very difficult challenge if they have not lived their life to the fullest.

As a son or daughter, you have the opportunity to be a blessing to your parents during this time. Encourage them and tell them what they did right. Affirm them in their old age and let them know what a blessing they are to you. Call them. Your voice of encouragement will be a strength for them during this time. Let them know they're not forgotten and remind them of all the good they have done.

In affirming your parents, you also need to plan how to take care of them in their old age. You may not have big financial resources but you can offer what you do have to assist them. Include them in holiday festivities, your activities, visit with them, and invite them to lunch. All of these actions will speak volumes to your parents. Your willingness to affirm them will reassure them that they are not forgotten nor forsaken late in life.

Ask Their Advice

Proverbs 23:22 states, "Hearken unto thy father that begat thee, and despise not thy mother when she is old." The older your parents become, the more wisdom and knowledge they acquire from life. In fact, your parents are filled with treasures! They may not know how to send text messages or how to work on the computer but they are loaded with experience. And what they do know, they would love to share with you.

If you will take God's Word to heart and listen to your parents in their golden years, you will discover a treasure chest full of golden advice from their years of accumulative life experiences. Asking for your parents' advice will also help affirm their value because they will feel validated in having something they can still contribute. This will go a long way in giving them purpose in their later years, especially if they know their advice and wisdom is appreciated and treasured.

One thing your parents may enjoy sharing with you are stories from the past. You can ask them about how they grew up and what they experienced. These conversations will be valuable to you as well because once your parents pass away, you will no longer be able to ask them these things. So take advantage of the time remaining and ask them about their past. Look at these conversations as a treasure hunt — each conversation provides an opportunity to discover more and more treasures about the past and your family history.

Seniors may also become forgetful. If your parents tend to forget things, that's ok. You don't have to tell them over and over that they already told you something. They may really think they're telling you something for the first time! Just listen to them, love on them, and let them communicate. That is truly a gift you can give your mom and dad in their old age.

Invest in Your Own Future

If you want to be remembered and cared for in your old age, start remembering and caring for your elderly parents now. When you care for your mom and dad, you are investing in your own future. You are honoring them, and that honor will come back to you from your kids later in life. It may not always be easy, but make the decision to show honor to the elderly. God will bless you for it!

The opportunity to sow into your elderly parents only comes once. After they've passed, you will never have the opportunity to care for them again. Listen to them and let them speak. Acknowledge their feelings and be kind. If they complain, extend compassion and grace. Show love to them, give them attention, and plan to make something special for them. Let this time with them be memorable.

By planting the right kinds of seeds into the relationships with your elderly parents, you are creating a good harvest for your future. Remembering your parents in their old age provides you with an opportunity to affirm them and ask for their advice. By honoring them, including them, and treasuring them, you will grow closer to your parents in this special season of life. When they do pass on from this earth, you will be able to reflect upon this time with gratitude for the memories you made with them and for the seeds you planted into your own future.

STUDY QUESTIONS

**Study to shew thyself approved unto God, a workman that needeth
not to be ashamed, rightly dividing the word of truth.
— 2 Timothy 2:15**

1. Galatians 6:7 explains the divine law of seedtime and harvest: "Be not deceived; God is not mocked: for whatever a man soweth, that shall he also reap." What kinds of seeds are you sowing into your elderly parents?

2. Galatians 6:7 reminds us, "Be not deceived; God is not mocked." Have you ever made excuses for your behavior, thinking your actions wouldn't ever catch up with you?

3. Proverbs 23:22 states, "Hearken unto thy father that begat thee, and despise not thy mother when she is old." What kind of attitude do you have towards your elderly parents? Do you treasure their wisdom or do you disregard their counsel?

PRACTICAL APPLICATION

> But be ye doers of the word, and not hearers only,
> deceiving your own selves.
> —James 1:22

Improve your relationships with your elderly parents by planting the right kinds of seeds in their old age.

1. How would you like to be treated when you are old? Are you treating your elderly parents the way you would like to be treated?

2. What can you do every day to make your elderly parents feel valued and connected?

3. What are your parents' favorite stories or anecdotes from the past? Have you considered making a family journal to record some of their nuggets of wisdom?

www.ingramcontent.com/pod-product-compliance
Lightning Source LLC
Chambersburg PA
CBHW071759020426
42331CB00008B/2326